RED Hot Teaching

21 "Yuck to Yay" Tools for Classroom Control

Linda Cordes

DEDICATION

This book is lovingly dedicated to Valerie, Veronica, Kairo, Gavino, and Bobby, my greatest sources of inspiration.

As promised in 1970, this book is gratefully dedicated to Anna Marie Roschitz, my seventh grade English teacher and RED Hottie before her time.

And, of course, this book is dedicated to you for finding it and using the tools within to unleash your inner hottie to make the world an even more awesome place in which to live, laugh, love, and learn.

CONTENTS

ACKNOWLEDGMENTS

I began this book in the summer of 2004, while strolling along the sunny beaches of Daytona. I continued to write bits and pieces over the next ten years. My best writing took place in crowded coffee shops, mom-and-pop diners, and salty-air piers overlooking the ocean. So, I must give credit to all the baristas, waiters, and waitresses who served up food and drink to fuel my reflection upon the craft of teaching. Most especially, I thank Everet who served me even more encouragement than coffee, and I drank a lot of coffee.

At times, I stumbled around to find the words to share this message. Sometimes I almost gave up, but each time, my good friend, Peggy Mulvihill, cracked the whip. "Girl, why isn't this in the hands of teachers yet? Stop procrastinating and get it done." Thank goodness for my ex-English teacher/drill sergeant/writing buddy!

Finally, I had completed this book, or so I thought. I have to thank my editor and sister, Susan Farley. After reading the few stories about how I used the tools, she wisely advised me to share a story for every tool. That sent me back to the beach to write more stories.

I have my mega-talented daughter, Valerie Castro, to thank for creating the whimsical winking Red Hot Teacher Logo. She is always and forever my favorite artist. Likewise, I am grateful to my grandson, Kairo Smith. His "Yuck to Yay" drawing at the end of this book sums up the student perspective on classroom controlling teachers.

Of course, I thank all my students over the years. They have taught me so much more than they will ever know. I learned the most from those who challenged me the most. I won't mention names, but if you are reading this, you know who you are. Thank you.

I thank all my fellow colleagues over the years who have listened to me on my soap box with "atta girl" reinforcements. A special thank you to every one of you who told me that I should write a book, or at least run the school. You gave me courage and reason to write this for you.

To all of the above, and so many more – thank you, thank you, thank you!

INTRODUCTION

Thank you for finding this book. You are a teacher. You love learning. You hold within you enormous power and passion. You impact the depth and direction of many lives on a daily basis.

So, how do you feel about that? Are you comfortable with this power? Do you use your power? Or are you too encumbered with lesson plans, extra duties, technology, professional development, data and testing, district mandates, etc.? Are you frustrated with out-of-control students who don't want to learn? Do you sometimes wish you had a magic wand to wave around and make all the crazy stuff go away, so you could finally just teach? Would you like to have teaching be easy, fun, and joyful again?

Whether you are a bright, shining newbie, or an "oldie but goodie," 21 RED Hot Teaching Power Tools gives you a bag full of tricks that work. Yes, really work for you. Try just one tool in this book and you will immediately unleash your power to focus your attention on priorities, so that you can quickly and easily knock out lesson plans, grade student work, and manage mounds of data, while gaining student cooperation and taking control of your classroom and your life!

The truth is we teachers own the greatest opportunity to influence the minds and hearts that will create and shape the future of our world. We could use a little help here! That's why, after thirty-three years of passion-driven instruction in a variety of classrooms with thousands of students and hundreds of teachers, this book has evolved to give you what you need to fire up your power and leverage it, as you joyfully master each awesome task you take on, beginning now.

Each segment of this book gives you:

- One short, easy to read and follow tool

- Inspirational related quote

- Brief explanation of how the tool works

- A real-life, personal example of the tool in action

- Suggestions for how to start using the tool immediately

- Suggestions for how to introduce the tool with students

- Reflection questions for journaling and evaluating how well the tool is working for you

You can be sure that what you get in this book is not the same old strategies disguised with fancy new names. In fact, there is no other book like this that will cut to the chase and address what really drags you down, holds you back, and burns you out. This is all the stuff that no one else will talk about in professional development. And now, here it is for you. So, turn the page and begin!

HOW TO USE THIS BOOK

Included in this book, are 21 RED Hot Power Tools. What are RED Hot Power Tools?

They are tools that engage and ignite the "whole teacher." Yes, you have a fantastic mind, and your mind is one part of a magnificent, energetic system that also includes your body, heart, and soul. When all four of these components are balanced and aligned, and you deliberately work them together, you are RED Hot! You create phenomenal outcomes!

RED Hot Power Tools align your energetic system and empower you to deliberately work all parts of your system together, in sync. No other professional development will do this for you. Wow, this is so amazingly awesome!

Imagine being in total control of yourself and your classroom, no matter what outside negative factors are thrown at you! You have got to try this.

Here are three different ways to get started. Select the level that suits you.

Level 1: Play With Fire (1 week)

This level is suggested if you are curious and want to try out samples of the tools.

Skim through the following pages and select a tool that you want to try.

Read that section thoroughly and commit to using the tool for a week.

Begin every day rereading the section that describes the tool. End every day journaling about your experience.

After a week, select another tool to practice.

Get ready! The spark you feel is your indicator light. You are ready for the next level.

Level 2: Get the Daily Fire Going (21 days)

This level is suggested if you'd like to try all the tools before you decide which ones you want to delve further into and master.

Begin with the first tool and spend a day on each one. Don't worry if you miss a day; just keep progressing through the tools in order. Some of the work and thought required in using the earlier tools paves the way for the understanding and effectiveness of using the later tools. It may take you longer than 21 days, and that is okay.

Begin each day reading the section that describes the tool for the day. Follow the "Do It" suggestions and complete the journal exercise at the end of the day.

By the time you complete your trial of all 21 tools, you'll know which ones you want to go back and master. Then you will no doubt want to join Linda in the RED Hot Teachers Lounge.

Level 3: RED Hot for Life (21 weeks)

This level is for you if you're sick and tired of feeling like no matter what you do, it's just getting harder and harder to do what you love to do – teach. You are looking for change that will last, and you are willing to invest your time and energy wisely into a self-directed personal development program that you monitor and control for yourself.

Begin with the first tool and progress through all the tools in order, spending one week on each tool. Start off each day with your journaling and rereading of the tool you are working on. Follow the suggestions for each tool. End each day with the journal exercise.

If you really want to understand and leverage your whole energy system, it is highly recommended that you join the RED Hot Teachers Lounge now!

No matter which level you choose, there is always support for you in the **RED Hot Teachers Lounge**, a website set up just for you and other like-minded hotties to find more help. Additional resources include blackline masters, videos, recorded teleseminars, and even more, as Linda adds new material. You will even be able to access live training on-site or at home with opportunities to get your burning questions answered by Linda Cordes, herself.

Check at http://www.REDHotTeaching.com now for information on how to get daily support as you work your way through each tool.

RED Hot Power Tool #1: Your RED Hot Journal

"Isn't it mysterious to begin a new journal like this? I can run my fingers through the fresh clean pages but I cannot guess what the writing on them will be." Maud Hart Lovelace

You may think of journaling as a means of describing the "what was" and the "what is." In other words, telling your story the way you see it as it unfolds.

Consider putting a twist on your journal. Make it a RED Hot Power Tool for telling your story the way you intend it to be. The key word here is "intend." Please note, you are never "in want" of anything. Want implies that it is beyond your reach. You must know that everything is not only within your reach, but within you.

How It Works

You will journal twice a day, morning and evening. In the morning, before you start your day, take just five minutes to write your intentions for the day in your journal. You might include your to-do list (the proactive steps you will take to turn difficult situations into opportunities).

In the evening, before bedtime, pull out your journal. Reread the morning entry and respond to your earlier thoughts. What are your positive results (positive only) for the day? What proof of personal growth can you document? List *"A-ha!"* moments that occur as you think about your positive results. What next step will you take tomorrow? What positive thought do you want to start off with tomorrow?

Before I released this book, I wrote the journal entry below to myself as "me writing back to me" to complete this project and get it into your hands.

The sole purpose of this journal entry was to inspire myself. You can imagine how ecstatically I am jumping up and down as you read the words that follow.

January 1, 2014

Dear Linda,

Woo hoo!

Twenty-one days ago, on December 12, 2013, you set out to complete the additions and edits to RED Hot Teaching. *I know you are smiling as you read this. A new year begins today, and you are releasing your best work ever.*

Finally, teachers have access to real tools. They can pick them up and get immediate results! Finally, they are able to stop reacting to overwhelming circumstances and start creating empowering circumstances. They can now move beyond putting out fires to lighting fires.

It took a little time to discover. It took some years of researching, implementing, and failing. Yes, failing. In fact, the failing is what led to the frustration that spiraled into overwhelming self-doubt and even hopelessness. Remember how discouraged you became? So discouraged that you reached a breaking point where you were ready to throw in the teaching towel. Thank goodness you did not.

Thank goodness, as always, in desperation you birthed a desire. You made a request. The answers began to trickle in.

The answers did not come from any professional development. In fact, you discovered they were right here and easily accessible as you learned to look through different lenses. It seemed incredulous that such simple yet profound ideas would really work. They did. Every time you used them, you saw the earth move. Earth you thought would never budge. So amazing! You had to share this stuff!

But what would other teachers think? Would they balk? Where was the research? What districts were using this? What were their results? How did this align with best practices? Was there proof this would raise test scores? Why wasn't anyone else talking about this? "Hmm…," you thought, "maybe they're not ready for this."

You kept it to yourself and just quietly went about learning and developing and growing these new "tools" on your own, by yourself. Your teaching life got happier and happier. Mondays brought joy and excitement. Fridays brought reflection and planning.

It did not matter that everyone else was stuck in the muck. Accreditation issues, threats of dismissal, school shootings, accountability fears, angry parents, disruptive students, dismally low test scores, budget cuts. It all seemed so overwhelming and hopeless to others. But you found the light. You learned how to let it go. You learned how to release the struggle. You learned how to navigate downstream in an upstream world. Other teachers around you were floundering, while you were flourishing. Nope, it just didn't matter that everyone else was stuck in the muck. Or did it?

Other teachers noticed your success, but chalked it up to, "That's just you. That's just Linda." Wow, if only they knew. If only they believed. You didn't make this up. You didn't invent it. You didn't get paid to research it. It just came to you because you asked the Universe for inspiration and strength to face your challenges. You were a ready student. The Universe opened up to become your teacher. Your knowledge and insight grew and grew in spurts, in leaps, in bounds. It grew too big, too powerful to contain. It popped out everywhere – in conversations, coaching, blogging, even a first book. It does matter. Teachers do get this. Teachers do understand. All the yuck is shifting to yay!

And now? It is ready. Here it is. <u>RED Hot Teaching</u>. It is completed. It is edited. It is viral! Millions of teachers thank you for sending out the message about what "really" happens in classrooms. They embrace the tools that finally allow them to create classes they control so that they can do what they love to do. Teach! Thank you, thank you, thank you!

Your ever present self,

Linda

Do It

Make it your intention to purchase a journal and special pen or pencil today.

Set your new writing materials in a place where you will see them and be able to write in the morning and evening. You may even want to carry your journal with you.

Write in your journal every morning and night for the remainder of the days you practice with the 21 tools.

Journal at the End of the Day

Write a note to yourself as you, writing back to yourself, today. Date your entry 21 days from today. You can explain how you feel after trying the 21 RED Hot Power Tools and the changes that you have experienced. You are setting some intentions here. Be powerful!

As you use each new tool over the remaining 20 days, you will get suggestions for what to journal about at the end of the day. You can continue to write your daily intentions in your morning journal entries.

RED Hot Power Tool #2: Check-In Partner

"If you hang out with chickens, you're going to cluck, and if you hang out with eagles, you're going to fly." Steve Maraboli

Welcome to RED Hot Teaching! It's time to find your eagles and get to flying!

How It Works

As you learn about and start using these fabulous RED Hot Power Tools, it will make it even more meaningful if you have a like-minded buddy to commit to the same challenge. You can encourage and cheer each other on. When you have an exciting *A-ha!* moment, you can call or text them and they will totally get it! You can make it even more fun by developing your own system for how you will communicate on a daily basis to share and compare your experiences. Any time you are taking on a self-transformation project, it is helpful to have both a coach and a check-in partner to help you stay on track.

As I write this, I chuckle. I am scratching away to meet a completion deadline I set with my check-in partner! I've been using a check-in partner ever since I hatched the concept of RED Hot Teaching. It's funny how my partner found me, or how we found each other.

One day I was reading favorite quotes online and I ran across the clucking chickens and soaring eagles quote. (See the quote at the beginning of this tool section.) I wrote it in my journal. As I thought about that quote, I realized I was clucking and I wanted to soar. In a fleeting moment, I made a wish to find an eagle. Just one, I thought. Just one person who would understand the schemes and dreams I was forming around my life purpose.

A week later, out of the blue, I received a phone call from a former colleague and friend. We had drifted apart and three or more years had passed since we had last communicated. She invited me to meet for coffee once a week to engage in a book study. She introduced me to a marvelous book to spark our creative genius.

Yay! I had found my eagle. Since then, we meet regularly to share our lives, our dreams, and our writing projects. I thank my good friend and check-in partner for holding me accountable and, more importantly, for encouraging me to complete the words you are reading right now. A check-in partner is a must. You need your co-eagle. Go get one now.

Do It

Determine who will be your check-in partner. More than one is okay.

Make sure you both sign up to join the RED Hot Teachers Lounge.

Determine a daily time to check in, and determine what it will look like. (Call, text, meet for coffee?)

Use these or similar questions to guide your discussion:

- What happened when you tried the tool?

- If you did not try the tool, what happened that prevented you from using the tool?

- What did you like about the tool?

- What will you do to make the tool fit you better?

- How will you use this tool with students?

- What support would you like to have in using this tool in the future?

Journal at the End of the Day

Who is your partner? When and where will you meet? What questions will you use to guide your check-in? If you do not yet have a partner, brainstorm now and make a list of possible people you can approach. Plan to tell them about the eagle quote!

RED Hot Power Tool #3: Pocket Mentor

*"A **mentor** is someone who sees more talent and ability within you, than you see in yourself, and helps bring it out of you."* Bob Proctor

There's nothing quite like carrying your personal guru around in your pocket or purse. Your very own pocket mentor. I'm talking about packing an inspirational book along with you wherever you go. It is a constant, comforting reminder to stay on your chosen path of focus.

How It Works

You may already have a favorite author or book that speaks to you and inspires you toward your goals. When you carry it with you, it is a physical as well as mental support to keep you focused on your priorities. When you begin to feel doubtful or frustrated, or otherwise drained of your usual enthusiastic mojo, you know you have your inspirational mentor at hand. All you have to do is pull him/her out and read!

Over the years, I have acquired a host of pocket mentors. I keep them together on a shelf and carry only one at a time – well, sometimes more! I love my mentors! I've marked some of my books with favorite words that speak to specific priorities in my life. I know you will find this pocket mentor tool fun and helpful.

Ask my oldest grandson. He can tell you who my pocket mentors are. I carry their books around with me wherever I go. I listen to their CDs in the car, and listen to them over and over as I drive around. I quote them in conversation. I refer to them on a first name basis. If they walked up to me in public, I would grab them and greet them with a great big hug. My mentors are that dear to me.

The best advice I can give you is to grow a list of such mentors. I started in the year 2003 by making a list of ten people I most wanted to meet. Using this word "meet" loosely allows me to include close encounters of the written, audio, and video kind. It makes all mentors accessible. There are no limits to time and space with this definition!

I'm calling out two of my mentors, Wayne and Abraham, right now because they most impacted my work on this book. They have an uncanny way of popping up for inspiration and direction just when I need them the most. What is even more intriguing to me is the way they show up as a pair to give me a double whammy!

In the summer of 2004, I came across Wayne Dyer's <u>Your Erroneous Zones</u> while browsing in a second-hand bookstore in Daytona, Florida. I flipped through it, bought it, and stuffed it in my bag. I had planned to read it later while basking on the sunny beach. An unexpected chain of events began unraveling, and I just didn't take time for basking. I carried Wayne around for the rest of the summer, but didn't crack him open. Not once. He just remained quietly waiting at the bottom of my bag. At the end of the summer, I tossed the bag to the back of my bulging closet.

Then, for no apparent reason, he resurfaced in August, 2006, just in time for the first day of back-to-school professional development. That morning before school, I was digging through the closet to find a pair of shoes to match my new outfit. I found them. There they were, right next to the bag I had tossed there two years before. I liked the look of that bag and remembered how much I could stuff into it. I rescued it and decided to take it with me that day.

When I arrived at PD, I dived into the bag to find a pen. Not finding one, I dumped everything, and out spilled Wayne. Another teacher snatched up the book. She was attracted to the title and the picture of Wayne in his "red-hot shorts." Her comment was, "Oh, I heard about this. Can I borrow it?" Even though I knew I'd probably never see the book again, I willingly handed it over. I was headed to the bookstore for a book and coffee treat later in the day. I made a mental note to look for a replacement copy or something better.

By the time I got to the store, I was pleased to discover that Wayne had many more recent books and I reached up high to pull one down. Instead, another book flew down from God only knows where, hit me on the head, and landed at my feet. I stooped to pick it up. <u>Ask and It Is Given: Learning to Manifest Your Desires</u>, by New York best-selling authors Esther and Jerry Hicks. There it was, the teachings of Abraham, forward written by none other than Wayne Dyer.

Hmm... so I guessed this was Wayne's way of telling me to read Abraham's book first. So I did. From that first book, I kept reading all and everything I could find by Esther, Jerry, Abraham, and Wayne. Of course, I added them to my list of influential people I wanted to meet in person.

Fast forward. I learned that Wayne and Esther and Abraham planned to meet up in Anaheim in November, 2013, for an open-to-the-public discussion. I knew I would be in on this conversation, and so I was. I purchased a ticket to listen in, via a webcast. Phenomenal! This was just the shot-in-the-arm inspiration I needed to pick up my pen and continue to write the stories to complete this book you are now reading.

My mentors do not cater specifically to educators. In fact, I have heard each one denounce the education they received for failing to teach them what really mattered most to their growth and development as a whole person. (The reason I am so compelled to write this book you are now reading!)

You will never hear them mentioned in any other "professional development." You will not find their teaching referred to in any educational journals. You will not find their books listed in any educational resource catalogs. You will not find their books on the shelves in your school's professional library. No book studies are forming among your colleagues to study their teachings.

Yet their message is profoundly essential to the very root of personal learning and growth. I can honestly tell you that because of my mentors – Jerry, Esther, Abraham, and Wayne – I was granted insight and curiosity to venture beyond accepting the worn-out status quo "reality" of the mediocre and failing school systems. Their teachings pushed me to think beyond the experience of a "professional" view and to open my mind to allow limitless possibilities. I came to understand the role I played in creating the status quo. More importantly, I came to understand that I have a choice to create beyond that status quo, to catalyze a whole new "status flow."

Now, I wish the same for you. If you are reading this, you are in the exact space and time to create your own list of mentors. Start now. Even one will make a difference in your life. You will be amazed at the dimension and clarity they will add to your understanding of "reality."

Go ahead. Get ready. When the student is ready, and you are ready, the mentor arrives.

Are you giddy with this thought? Today, you meet your mentor!

Do It

Today, you visit a library or bookstore.

You tell the librarian or clerk that you are looking for an inspirational book and ask them to steer you toward the appropriate aisle. Thank them and dismiss them!

Now, just browse freely with the intention of being open to whatever images and/or words catch your interest. (This is the magic step that will bring the right mentor to you.)

When you find the one that is calling you, check it out or buy it.

You now have your pocket mentor.

Journal at the End of the Day

Who is your pocket mentor? Describe how your pocket mentor "selected you."

What insight did your pocket mentor divulge to you today?

How will you use this tool with students?

RED Hot Power Tool #4: Gratitude List

"No matter who you are, no matter where you are, no matter what your current circumstances, the magic of gratitude will change your entire life!" Rhonda Byrne

Imagine what will happen when you harness the power of this magic called gratitude! Imagine how your classroom will look and feel when you begin to feel conscious gratitude for every aspect? Yes, every aspect. Keep reading and find out how to use this tool!

How It Works

Simply make a list of all the things that you are grateful for. Consider all areas of your life. Delve into situations that appear unpleasant and unwelcome on the surface. What can you find to be thankful for about each one? What about the difficult people you deal with each day? What opportunities and lessons are they providing to you? What challenges can you be grateful for because you are learning new skills that break through the limiting boundaries of your old comfort zones?

It is really easy to find gratitude among the roses and lollipops, but what about the more unlikely places? The more you challenge yourself to find gratitude in unlikely places, the more you will enjoy and benefit from using this tool. Each time you do this, you will strengthen your immunity to the negative, while inviting more positive roses and lollipops into your experience.

Each time you do this, try to list at least ten things you are grateful for. By the time you get to seven or sooner, you will feel your mood shifting and your energy rising.

Here is an example of how I used this tool one summer, while on vacation. (Yes, these tools work anytime, anywhere!!)

Do you ever feel so low and discouraged that you want to slap those happy, chirpy people flitting around telling you to think positively? I do. At first thought, the circumstances I am focusing upon seem undeniably harsh and "real." Does this happen to you? This, my friend, is the best time to write gratitude statements! The secret to making it work is to be easy with yourself by moving from generic to designer.

Here is what I mean by "generic to designer." It doesn't work to start out telling yourself things you don't believe. It does work to start out with very general statements of possibility, and gradually transition to more specific statements of what you desire. So, you start off with general statements that do not require much emotional attachment. Then, gradually increase the specific details of your statement and feel your mood shift from discouraged to hopeful. This is when you see the light at the end of your tunnel.

One hot July day, I was facing the defeated feeling of more month than money. I was fearful that I would not be able to pay all my bills. I took out my gratitude book and here is what I wrote:

1. I am grateful I am not teaching summer school because I have time to figure something out about these bills.

2. I am grateful I am open to money flowing to me.

3. I am grateful there are options I have not yet considered because one or more of them will work.

4. I am grateful there are people who need my gifts and talents.

5. I am grateful I have skills that are helpful to other people.

6. I am grateful for the extra $1000 that is coming to me this week.

7. I am grateful I can help someone and they will be so happy to exchange $1000 for my help.

8. I am grateful I am always able to pay my bills.

9. I am grateful I am a money magnet.

10. I am grateful I am the creator of my reality.

After I wrote these statements, I closed my journal and began my day. It was summer, so I went outside to water my garden. A school bus rolled by and then another. I barely noticed them. As the third and fourth passed, one behind the other, I thought to myself, "Hmm... summer school, maybe I should be there making money."

Then the fifth and sixth rolled by, a little louder. The noise was not from the bus. The noise was from children yelling and shouting out the rolled-down windows. I chuckled to myself because that was my reminder of why I was not teaching summer school! I laughed a little louder and began to relax and enjoy the warm sunshine and think about the fun I would have that afternoon taking my grandson to the swimming pool.

Then it dawned on me. Six busses. I wondered if another would roll by to make it seven.

(Seven is a special number to me. The occurrence of the number seven always tells me something magically cool is about to happen.)

As I rolled up the hose and listened to my dog barking at the traffic, there it was. Magic bus seven. Oh yeah, something good was going to happen and I gave my worry over to possibility. I ran inside and upstairs to my office to pull out a fresh piece of paper. I began to make a list of things I could do to make some quick bucks.

Here's the list:

- Garage sale

- e-bay auction

- pawn something

- Sell stuff on Craigslist

- Part-time job

- Mow lawns

- Tutor

Tutor? I stopped. Yeah! I have done this before and convinced clients to pay me up front. This could work. I logged in to Craigslist and entered my ad, three ads actually.

I was feeling pretty good now!

I packed up the pool bag and headed out to pick up my grandson for swimming. As soon as I pulled into the swimming pool parking lot, my phone rang.

You guessed it. A tutoring customer. A tutoring customer with six more friends! She had her daughter and six more kids who needed some "summer enrichment." Would I consider doing a class and lowering my price per child? My math brain kicked in. Let's see, $25 times two hours, times seven kids, times four weeks comes to $1400!

I let her know I would think it over and get back to her. Think it over, I did. I donned my shades and dug out my pen and notebook to plan. A four-week math camp with puzzles, games, crafts, competitions, prizes, and goodies. The best part? I would make my $1000, with extra to purchase prizes, and make seven kids really smart and happy!

I was so excited that I had to force myself to swim seven pool lengths, dive seven times, and go down the water slide seven times. My grandson was amazed by his granny's sudden burst of energy. Finally, I called the customer back, and we agreed upon the terms and set a schedule in place. All the while, I was appreciating the time I took that morning to write my gratitude statements.

You just have to use this tool. It works!

Do It

On a piece of paper, take time right now to write down ten things for which you are grateful. Super-power your list by making statements that each begins, "I am grateful for ... because ...."

If you are keeping a journal as part of this 21-day challenge, choose a page at the end of the journal and begin your list there. Every day, add five to ten more gratitude statements.

Before you journal tonight; reread your list.

Journal at the End of the Day

Write about your experience with this tool. What benefits did you experience? How would you teach students to use this tool? When would you encourage them to use it?

RED Hot Power Tool #5: Rewrite the Book

"History will be kind to me for I intend to write it." Winston
Churchill

*"Civilization had too many rules for me, so I did my best to rewrite
them."* Bill Cosby

Remember those great books that had empty pages at the end so
you could write your own ending? And how about those books that
had one version of the story written on the odd-numbered pages
reading forward, and another version of the story written on the
even-numbered pages when you flipped the book over and read it
from the back, upside down, and forward? The story was totally
different depending on how you held the book and how you
"looked at it." You got to choose your own perspective on the
story.

It's like this in real life, and the versions are unlimited! It's like this
in your classroom. You can write your story from different
perspectives. Why not choose one that serves you? Why not
choose one that serves your purpose?

How It Works

Think about an issue in your outer world that you would like to
"rewrite." Think about the way you would like it to be, rather than

how you perceive the current "reality."

Write a description of how you want the new reality to be. Never mind how "reasonable" you think it may be. This is your mind and you can create your own thoughts for your own reasons. In the new story, what are you doing? What are you saying? How are you feeling? What are the other characters in your story doing, saying, and feeling?

The first time I tried this tool, I was totally blown away by the dramatic difference it made for a student named "Darrell." You have to understand that Darrell was my "challenge of the year." You know how there is always that one student who never lets up. The other teachers on my team sarcastically referred to Darrell as "your favorite."

They knew by my daily complaints and his daily stories about me that he was anything but "my favorite." It wasn't just me. Darrell caused chaos and disruption in every one of his classes. His behavior just seemed to escalate as his "meds" wore down, and my class was the last class before his trip to the nurse for the next dose. I was at my wit's end one day, and so I sat down to rewrite the story of failure and disruption for my friend Darrell.

"Once upon today, the bell rang for fourth hour to begin. I glanced down the hall, expecting to see Darrell lollygagging around the drinking fountain, but he was nowhere in sight. I turned my attention to greeting the class as I entered the classroom. To my surprise, there was Darrell sitting in his front-row seat, busily working on his "do now." He glanced up and smiled briefly at me, and then returned to his work. Though it took me by surprise, it was a pleasant surprise. I couldn't help wondering what magic had come over him. Then, I realized that I had written this story, and so it had come to pass."

The passage you just read is the actual story I wrote that day when I was ready to throw in the towel on Darrell. The very next day, just before I met with Darrell's class, I pulled out this same story and reread it. With no further thought, I scurried off to pick up the class from lunch.

There was Darrell, waiting for me. He popped up from the cafeteria table and blurted out, "I have to go to my locker now so I can get to class on time today." I started to object, but something about the urgency in his voice provided me with faith that he was on the up and up.

"Okay," I said, "I'll see you in your seat in five minutes." Can you guess where he was five minutes later? Yep, in his seat. It almost felt a little eerie in light of "the story" I'd written, but I was liking it!

It got even better. Darrell announced to the class, "I'm gonna be the first one done with this "do now." He was. Then he proceeded to further amaze his classmates by concocting an extremely creative way to solve the problem. We dubbed it "Darrell's Dazzle of the Day."

Darrell was on a roll. The next part of class was collaboration with a partner. Usually, Darrell had to collaborate with himself, but he requested to work with another student named Stewart. I didn't want to break his spirit, so I agreed.

I got busy circulating to other groups of students, and it was ten or fifteen minutes before I got around to Stewart and Darrell. I couldn't believe my eyes. There was Stewart, snoozing away, while Darrell was completely absorbed with creating a unique solution to an open-ended problem. I gave him a huge grin, thumbs-up, and moved on.

By the time the class was ready to share aloud their solutions, Darrell was sitting there, looking pretty smug. I gave him another grin, and he popped out of his seat to come whisper in my ear, "Let me go last; I want to be the grand finale."

Do It

Identify an issue in your current physical reality that you would like to be different.

If you had a magic, red, sparkly, transforming wand to wave over it, how would it really look? What would really happen? What would you really say and do? How would other people in your story respond to you?

After considering how to answer these questions, write an account of the new story. Now, go live the rest of your day and watch what happens!

Journal at the End of the Day

So, here is where you record what happened after rewriting your story. What changes did you notice, or not? How do you feel about this? What other stories will you rewrite?

RED Hot Power Tool #6: Reframe

"When you change the way you look at things, the things you look at change." Wayne Dyer

Wouldn't it be great if you could take every negative thing and turn it into something positive?

Sounds great! Sounds impossible? When you continue to look at the negative from the same perspective it will remain the same negative. The trick is to change your perspective. Assume the opposite. OK, so here is a great tool for doing just that. I call it REFRAMING!

How It Works

Brainstorm around a topic that is concerning you. Write down everything that comes to mind.

Reread what you have just written. Circle everything you wrote that is positive (makes you feel good).

Get out a fresh piece of paper. Head it with your topic. Copy down all the positive things you circled from the other paper.

Now, look at each item you did not circle on the first paper and, one by one, restate them. (It will help to review how to use the restate tool. See Tool #12.)

As you restate your negative items, and you are satisfied that they now make you feel good, add them to your list of circled positives.

Are there things about teaching that you have come to dread? Lesson plans? Formal Observations? Cafeteria duty? "That" class?

One year, the teacher across the hall coined the term "Terrible Tuesday." She claimed that every Tuesday "all hell broke loose" and her class turned upside down with discipline problems and all sorts of craziness. It never failed. She expected it to happen, and it did.

It started in August after the first two really rough Tuesdays of the school year. She laughed and said, "Tuesdays are always bad." Then on Monday, she would say, "Get ready for tomorrow, Terrible Tuesday!" By the end of every Tuesday, as expected, she would poke her worn-out head in my door and say, "Well, what did I tell you?"

It irritated me that I had let her infect me with this negative thought pattern. One fifth, twenty percent of my week, was dreaded and destined to be terrible. I really had to fight this. I did not want to believe it. How could I deny the results of every Terrible Tuesday, as September rolled into October, and every Tuesday repeated the pattern?

Then it hit me. It was our own thinking and labeling that set us up every week for this repeat performance. Labels tell you what to expect, good or bad. Once you label something, then that is what you look for. That is what you prepare for. That is what you get. I was not happy with what I was getting, and it was time to reframe my thinking around Tuesdays.

I sat down, and this is the brainstorm that spilled out:

Terrible Tuesday

Thank God it's only one day a week

Terrible

Kids go crazy

Pat throws tantrums

Jacob has meltdowns

No Specials

Library day

Always rains

Attendance always good

Kids get disruptive when they forget their library books and can't check out another

I circled the positives. Then I got out a fresh piece of paper and rewrote all the positives.

Next, I looked at everything not circled, which was most of the list. One by one, I turned them into positive statements by looking for silver linings.

Here is what the new page looked like:

Terrific Tuesday

Library day

Attendance is good

This is my opportunity to make Tuesday the best day of the week

No specials give me opportunity to do our own special activities, like centers or fun projects

Now I can make a list of rainy day activities to share with other teachers

Pat and Jacob will love being the coordinators of Terrific Tuesday activities

Kids who forget books can check out books from my classroom library

This was my start. I was feeling much better, and I noticed as the dread dissipated, solutions appeared. My shifting thought energy moved me to inspired action. I pulled out a huge, oversized piece of construction paper and wrote "TERRIFIC TUESDAY," creating a sign.

I began posting the sign on my classroom door every Tuesday. My friend across the hall laughed. My kids asked what it meant. I told them every Tuesday we were going to look for the terrific things happening and make a public list. They thought this was really cool, and we started right off by putting down that Tuesday was Library Day. From there, the list grew and grew until it overtook the entire board. Eventually we had to devote a green spiral notebook with a page for each Tuesday. Our challenge was to increase the number of items on our list each Tuesday.

It was now difficult for kids like Pat and Jacob to feel bad on such an awesome day as Tuesday. By the end of February, we had so many reasons to like Tuesday that my friend across the hall was asking what ever happened to Terrible Tuesday.

We replaced it. We reprogrammed it. We reframed it. You can too.

Do It

Select an issue that you have been resisting or avoiding. Maybe it's a person with whom you have a disagreement, or a project you don't want to start.

Go through the steps listed above.

Note how you feel by the time you finish.

List any action steps that come to mind, and complete one immediately.

Journal at the End of the Day

Describe your experience with this tool. How did it help you? What other issues do you plan to reframe?

How will you teach students to use this tool? At what times will it be useful to your students?

RED Hot Power Tool #7: Seven Teacher Affirmations

"An affirmation is any statement that we make – whether positive or negative. If affirmations are used consistently, they become beliefs and will always produce results, sometimes in ways that we cannot even imagine." Louise Hay

How It Works

Create seven really great affirmations related to your goals as a teacher.

Write them down on an index card that you can carry with you, or keep the card in a prominent place where you will see it daily.

Remember to state your affirmations in the present tense.

Following are seven of my favorite Teacher Affirmations:

- I am so happy and grateful now that I view each student as an important person whom I inspire on the journey to discover and pursue unique passions to make the world a better place.

- I am so happy and grateful now that I spend 80% of my time on the 20% most important tasks.

- I am so happy and grateful now that I am a partner with the parents of my students.

- I am so happy and grateful now that I engage each student in self-directed learning.

- I am so happy and grateful now that I am learning to reflect and reframe.

- I am so happy and grateful now that I am learning to employ my emotions to empower my effort to achieve the results I desire.

- I am so happy and grateful now that I am doing daily practices to achieve the results I desire.

I had to keep my affirmations a secret around people who might poke holes in them. You, too, will hear people give all kinds of reasons why affirmations do not work. I am telling you right now the one important fact you need to know. When your beliefs match your affirmations, your affirmations work.

Let's say you affirm, "I am so grateful I am a size 7." Then, immediately you think, "Yeah, right! You'll never see that. You are too fat, too old, too...." Your affirmation does not match your beliefs. Furthermore, the intensity of your counter beliefs "outweigh" your affirmation. Your beliefs always win.

So, you have two choices for success. You can change your affirmation, or you can change your belief. How can you do this?

I always listen to my voice when I say the affirmation. If I do not convince myself and feel excited, I try to reword it so that it sounds more sincere and believable. I used to make affirmations about making money, but my beliefs revolved around the perceived "reality" of my teacher salary.

I kept rewording my statement until I came up with a believable affirmation:

The Universe is limitless; I am limitless; I have limitless access to limitless money; I am a money magnet to a limitless source of abundance.

I say "believable" because I was a math teacher for many years. I taught calculus. I totally understood and bought into the concept of infinity!

I began to say this out loud, in writing, and in my head when I went for walks. The more I said it, the more I believed it, and the more I created evidence to reinforce an even deeper belief.

Money started popping up everywhere.

Pennies on the floor.

Ten dollar bills in pockets of old coats.

Twenty dollar bills on the ground by abandoned gas pumps.

Hundred dollar checks from someone who wanted me to tutor their child.

Thirty thousand dollar raises from companies offering me new jobs

I love playing around with affirmations, wording and rewording them until I get them in balance with my beliefs. Here is an add-on you can use on any affirmation. It has a built-in quality that bridges the gap between your affirmation and belief.

I am so grateful I am _____ even better than I can now believe or imagine.

I get goose bumps just thinking what you can do with this one!

Oh, and the really, really, really cool part? The more you use your affirmations, the better you get. The better you get, the more evidence you create for yourself that they do work. In fact, over time, you will notice that your beliefs are shifting to match your affirmations! Oooh, what power you have now!

Do It

Write your seven affirmations. Feel free to use any of the ones I shared with you!

Read them out loud. Repeat and read them really loudly and like you really mean them!

Take them out three more times today and repeat them, reading them out loud, and really loudly.

Journal at the End of the Day

Write down your seven affirmations in your journal. How did it feel to read them really loudly and emphatically? Make a plan for when you will say your affirmations each day. Write down your plan in your journal.

RED Hot Power Tool #8: Visualize

"The reality you experience is the mirror image of your expectations." Deepak Chopra

I recall hearing someone in a lecture explain that worry is visualizing about what we don't want. How many times have you worried about something happening in the future (dreading Mondays, dreading "that class," dreading that observation next week, etc.)?

If you have participated in worry, then you already know how to visualize! Now, let's see how to make it work for you instead of against you!!

How It Works

Visualization is "seeing" what you want in your mind before and as you go for it.

Paint the picture, create the scene, and use the image to focus your direction. There are countless stories of famous people who became successful using visualization. From Oprah, to Tiger Woods, to Gandhi, to You. Setting your sight on where you want to be and what you want to achieve is a first and ongoing step to achieving big dreams.

Here are some suggestions to make your visualization more

effective:

- Close your eyes to help tune out distractions for greater focus.

- Think in color, vivid colors.

- Create and see signs with words or short phrases, arrows pointing the way.

- Include movement and action.

- Include yourself; "see" yourself.

- Repeat the same visualization often – maybe daily at the same time.

- Start off with a single picture; then, over time, continue to add more details and action to create a mind movie.

- Include all five senses. What do you smell, and taste, and feel?

- Include emotion and take time to dwell on the positive feelings.

- Look for actual pictures in magazines, newspapers and online to feed your mind images of what you want.

- Take photos of what you want and put yourself in the picture. (I have two great stories of how I "pictured" myself into the car I drive and the home I am buying.)

- Expect to get better the more you practice.

- Expect to really enjoy this more and more as you get better and better.

Now, how can you help kids with visualization? I use it to help kids reach academic and behavioral goals.

Believe it or not, kids are much more willing to use this strategy than adults. They are more closely in touch with their imaginations than adults!

Here is an example of how I used visualization to gain advantage and kick some academic butt at school.

One year, I coached my school's National Academic League Team. We spent weeks preparing questions and answers, and researching possible debate topics. We felt quite confident to meet each and every team — except for Washington Prep Academy. Washington was an elite college prep school, the only school in the district allowed to hold an academic GPA requirement. Washington had long-standing bragging rights for brutally and ridiculously outscoring every other school in the district in every academic competition. No one else ever even came close.

Three of my team members could attest to this from their prior year experience. Early in the season, long before we would come up against Washington, they began to tell horror stories. They recounted being so intimidated by Washington that they froze and couldn't even hit the buzzer. Washington racked up point after point as the fifteen minute clock ran out. After the whole awful ordeal, they realized that 90% of the questions were answered by the same boy on the Washington team.

As the dreaded encounter drew closer and closer, the talk continued and even began to escalate. I overheard comments like, "This is going to be embarrassing. They're gonna kill us." All of this fear-talk was eating away at our confidence.

We were down to the wire with only two days until we would oppose Washington head to head. One student actually asked if we could take a forfeit to avoid humiliation. Oh yeah! This was the perfect opportunity to visualize a victorious outcome! (Remember that the funny thing about worry is that most people fail to see it for what it really is. Worry is just visualizing what you do not want. Why not visualize what you do want. It feels so much better!)

It just so happened that two of our own team members were Washington Prep Academy rejects. In their own words, Jake and Taron told us how they were, "kicked out of Washington because we was bad and our grades suck." Maybe they did have challenging behavior and substandard grades, but they were also cream-of-the-crop intelligent and undeniably gutsy. They were my leaders and I could depend on them to rally the rest of the team to any challenge. Besides, they had a vested interest in kicking some vengeful butt.

I started out by asking the kids to consider turning their fear into fun. So what could we do to keep Washington from monopolizing the buzzer and racking up all those points?

I wanted them to start looking at circumstances differently to get different results.

I asked the kids to humor me and try something totally cool and just for fun. They agreed because every time I said, "Just humor me," they got to do something fun that other teachers wouldn't even consider.

Here is what I told them to do: "Now close your eyes and relax. Take three deep breaths. (I secretly set the timer for fifteen minutes.) See yourself sitting at the team table smiling, sitting straight up and confident, glancing at each other and exchanging knowing looks. Now look at the Washington team players. Smile at them. You are thinking, 'Good luck, guys. You'll need it. We have a surprise for you.'

"Now see your buzzer. See your hand. It is ready to hit the buzzer. See Mr. Richards asking the question and you hit the buzzer just as he speaks the last word. You see the stunned looks on the faces of the Washington team. You are smiling as you answer. Mr. Richards is saying, 'That is correct!'"

I repeated this over and over until each member had a turn hitting the buzzer and giving a correct answer. The time ticked on and on. Fifteen minutes was soon over. When the buzzer sounded, they all jumped in their seats and fell out laughing.

I asked them how it felt to hit the buzzer and answer the question in front of the Washington team. They needed to know what it felt like and what it looked like to beat Washington out of hitting the buzzer. They needed to know that they could see it and feel it.

Feeling and seeing what you want is the beginning of creating reality.

Through our follow-up conversation, it occurred to them that even if they couldn't beat Washington, they could certainly minimize the damage. The main thing they had to do was to just hit the buzzer! Of course, they wanted to know what to do if they hit the buzzer and didn't know the answer. So I gave them three strategies:

- Ask the emcee to repeat the question.

- Wait out the clock and give whatever answer popped into their heads.

- Wait out the clock and give the answer, "Chocolate jelly beans."

They all laughed at the last one. They began to see the advantage of stalling for time. First, it would break the momentum of the Washington team and throw them off guard. Secondly, it would run out the 15 minutes on the clock and give Washington less time to run up the score in their favor. It would show Washington that we were not afraid to answer and were not intimidated by their reputation.

When they started to focus on these strategies, they forgot about their fear of embarrassment. They decided that Jake would hit the buzzer on the spelling and grammar questions, and Taron would man the buzzer on all the other questions because they were the respective gurus. Excitement was growing. They even practiced hitting the buzzer with other stand-in students playing the part of the Washington team. One such practice session left them rolling on the floor as the frustrated Washington team begged for mercy.

Finally, it was game day. We huddled around the team table for a last minute pep-talk. "Everyone ready?" "Oh yeah! Bring it on!" We all threw our hands in the middle and shouted out, "Chocolate jelly beans!!" If Washington didn't know then, they were about to find out. Our team was about to give them a run for their money.

Of course, you know the strategy worked! Just as they had visualized, our team hit the buzzer first every time. Every time. Halfway through the round, my captain signaled for a time-out. When I approached the table, all they wanted to share with me was, "This is really working. Just like we saw it." They were so pumped. They returned to the competition.

What followed was amazing. Not only were they hitting the buzzer, but they were coming up with more and more correct answers! Their confidence reduced their stress and they were thinking more clearly, free of the former fear.

The judges were noticeably impressed. At the last break before announcing the final scores, two of the judges approached. They shook hands with each member of our team and told them how outstandingly they had performed. No other team had stood up to Washington in such a confident manner.

Well, long story short, our team didn't outscore Washington that day. But, on the other hand, our team did learn the phenomenal power of visualization.

When kids are grumbly or frustrated or acting out, I help them to focus their attention on achieving more positive goals by guiding them through a brief visualization session. I do this with a series of questions and suggestions.

I also consult with my good friend, Peggy Mulvihill, author of <u>Calm Kids</u>.

Do It – for Students

Do this with your student/students. Say the following:

"Close your eyes and take a deep breath in through your nose – 1,2,3,4.

"Blow out through your nose – 1,2,3,4. Relax your face and keep your eyes closed.

"Think about _____ (the academic or behavioral goal they are struggling to achieve, such as sitting like a learner).

"See yourself smiling. See the smile spreading across your face.

"See yourself sitting in your desk. Feel the chair underneath you and your feet flat on the floor.

"Notice the color of your shoes and the grey tiles on the floor under your desk.

"Your pencil is in your hand, etc." (You create the image that will help the child be successful for the specific situation.)

Do It – for You

Set an intention before you begin. You want to feel calmer. You want to feel more confident. You want to accomplish a goal, etc.

Create a scene or image of your intention that includes all of your senses.

Now, close your eyes and take three deep breaths.

Begin to think about the scene or image you created, and relax with the thoughts that flow around it for as long as it feels comfortable. If your mind strays, bring it back to your created scene until you feel relaxed and ready to come back to your day.

Open your eyes and say, "Thank you."

Journal at the End of the Day

Write about your experience with visualization. When do you think this would help you? When do you plan to use this tool again? How and when would you use this tool with students?

RED Hot Power Tool #9: The Conveyer Belt

"You cannot prevent the birds of sorrow from flying over your head, but you can prevent them from building nests in your hair."
Chinese Proverb

We cannot prevent negative and discouraging thoughts from entering our heads, but we don't have to let them take hold of our minds either!

This next tool that I call the Conveyer Belt will help you wave bye-bye to those negative and discouraging thoughts.

How It Works

Imagine the myriad of thoughts streaming through your mind are on a conveyer belt that passes through your head from left to right. As thoughts come through, you are going to notice how they make you feel.

If they please you, you'll allow your mind to suck them in and absorb them into the limitless pockets of your subconscious mind, where you can store them for later retrieval. When negative thoughts pass by, notice them and smile as you allow them in one ear and out the other. Wave goodbye to them if you wish.

Isn't it great to know that you are not with these negative thoughts! You don't have to fight them. You just let them flow in and out. And here's where it gets even better. You control the speed of your conveyer belt. So, when you catch yourself bombarded by self-doubting thoughts and you feel overwhelmed, just turn that sucker up! Then halt production and start your thought flow in a totally new direction!

I started teaching this tool to people who came to me stuck on a negative train of thought. I was visiting a friend and we got to talking about husbands. She was considering leaving hers because he was not meeting her expectations as a father.

She told me he was saying negative things to the kids, and she did not want them to grow up with those limiting thoughts. She was brought up that way, and she was determined her kids would have a different experience.

I asked her if she loved her husband. Of course, she did. But they were always fighting about the things he said to the kids.

I asked her if she knew about the conveyer belt. Of course, she did not. I began to describe the tool and explained how she could use it when her husband talked to the kids. She could imagine the conveyer belt passing through their home with her husband's words floating along on top of it. The good comments would jump off and the bad comments would pass on through the wall. She could react to the positive comments and ignore the negative comments.

She laughed at this and said she would give it a try.

A couple of weeks later, she called me, very excited, and told me she did use the conveyer belt. It worked! She said she added her own touches. Instead of her husband's words, she imagined little tiny figures of her husband.

The tiny husbands who said crazy things just got a wave goodbye. They shrunk down even smaller and passed on through the walls of their home. The tiny, positive, nurturing husbands were invited in. They grew large as life and sat down on the loveseat next to her. Wow! I really liked the way she personalized the tool!

46

I asked her what effect this tool was having on her husband. She revealed that the tool caused a break-through conversation. Because she released her need to verbally disapprove of his interactions with the kids, her husband relaxed enough to admit he did not have a clue how to raise the kids. He did not want to yell at them, or threaten and berate them. He just wanted them to be good, happy kids, and he wanted her to love him.

Then came the shocker. He told her that he wished he could be more "calm, like her." He even asked her to teach him how. What do you think she taught him first? The conveyer belt!

Do It

- Try this tool now, for about five minutes. Start up your conveyer belt and observe the thoughts that start flowing by.

- Try this tool later, while stuck in traffic, waiting in a checkout line, etc., and watch the effect it has on otherwise boring or negative situations.

- Try it at least three more times today.

Journal at the End of the Day

What did you experience as you used this tool? Explain how it felt to flip your conveyer belt switch to control your flow of thoughts. How did other people respond? Did you notice anything unusual?

How would you teach students to use this tool? When and where would you expect them to use it?

RED Hot Power Tool #10: The 17-Second Shift

"When you hold a thought for as little as seventeen seconds, the law of attraction kicks in. In other words, that's the combustion point where another matching thought joins in." Abraham Hicks

The trick here is to stay focused on one thought for 17 seconds! When you master this, you hold a powerful tool for shifting any pattern of thought that does not serve you.

How It Works

Hold a positive thought for 17 seconds.

If you can hold a positive thought for 17 seconds, more related thoughts will flood your mind. If you can keep this up for 68 seconds – that is, just four times the 17 seconds – you will totally shift your mood to positive.

Consider holding favorite thoughts such as a special person, pet, place to be, scene, food, thing to do, past event, future event, etc. I like to use this exercise for a few minutes prior to dealing with a difficult student, class, parent, or meeting I don't want to attend. Sometimes, I stop in the middle of class when I begin to feel a funky vibe starting up from a grumbly group of students.

Here's an example of how it went down one day when Monica and Stacy started to gripe about "all the work," and that "this is too hard," and "I wish they never made up this Algebra stuff." My old reaction would have been to snap back at them with some authoritarian remark about where Algebra came from and why they needed to learn it.

Instead, I just caught them where they were and joined in with, "Yeah. We could just work on times tables and stuff you already know. Imagine how easy that would be. We could just kick back and relax every day. Just think about that." And I stopped with a smile on my face and thought about their happy faces as I counted in my head, "14, 13...." By the time I got to zero, they were grinning and got back to work. I didn't even have to repeat with more 17-second intervals. Their energy had already shifted by.

Now, here is the added bonus to this exercise. Don't be surprised when I tell you right now that whatever you are holding in your thoughts for 68 seconds and feeling really good about, is likely to appear within your experience, sometimes immediately!

It may not be delivered in the same form you thought about, and you may not recognize it at first. It's nothing magical. It just appears.

It doesn't even matter if you are skeptical. This works anyway.

Got a minute and eight seconds? Want to instantly feel better? Try it right now!

Do It

- Do this now. Think about a favorite something and concentrate your focus for 17 seconds. Sometimes I count in my head to 17. On each number I see a flash of my favorite. If it is a person, I see each flash as a different expression, or in different outfits, or doing different things with me. It helps me focus more on the thought, rather than the counting. If you run out of flashes, just loop back through the same ones.

- Now do it again with some situation that has been troubling you. Flip the situation around and create a thought around a more positive outcome to the situation. Use this and focus upon it for 17 seconds. Repeat until you reach 68 seconds.

- Look for at least two more times today when you can use your tool.

Journal at the End of the Day

What did you experience as you used this tool? When did it come in handy today?

How would you teach this tool to students, and when would you want them to use it?

When would you use this tool in your classroom?

RED Hot Power Tool #11: Take Your Temperature

"Nothing can grow beyond your emotional response. Everything matches your Set-point of emotions on every subject that exists."
Abraham Hicks

You probably notice how good things happen when you feel good. So, it is important to know how you are feeling and to be able to raise that feeling at will whenever you want to do so.

How It Works

Use this scale of feelings to judge your "temperature." If you are attempting to motivate others or to be creative, it's important to make sure that your emotional temperature aligns with your intention. When you notice a struggle or feel emotionally drained, it just means that your emotions are mismatched and it's time to pull out other tools from your RED Hot repertoire.

Here is a scale I use.

+3	passionate, empowered, loving, knowing
+2	positive, expecting, believing
+1	hopeful
0	neutral, passive
-1	doubtful
-2	angry, frustrated, blaming
-3	fearful, powerless, overwhelmed, unworthy

When I first learned about the scale of emotions, I began to understand the power I had over my outcomes. I often heard, "You cannot change others; you can only change how you respond to them." That was great, but they still ticked me off! I still got all worked up and dragged into all kinds of drama where I did and said things that I later regretted.

Then this thermometer tool gave me the power to stop at the onset and intercept the oncoming emotion, sending it back so that I could replace it with another.

The first thing I did was just exactly what I am going to tell you to do. I carried a copy of the emotional scale around on an index card. I set timers on my cell phone and computer so I could stop to check my temperature. After the fourth alarm, my students wanted to know what was up.

I gave them a short explanation by writing the scale on the board. I invited them to join me. Now that my game was public, I had to step it up. I did not want my students to catch me down at level -2!

My awareness of my temperature actually made me choose my words and actions more consciously. I noticed that as I did this, I was creating a "transference of heat." My steady high temperature radiated enough positive energy for my kids to catch on. They were also choosing their words and actions more consciously. Everyone in the room was striving to be above 0 when the alarms sounded for temperature time.

Do It

Write the scale on an index card and carry it with you today. Periodically refer to the card and "take your temperature."

If you find your temperature has dropped, listen to your words and notice your thoughts. What are you and others around you saying and doing?

Use the Conveyer Belt or the 17 Second Shift. Then retake your temperature.

Has your temperature risen? Try the tool again and note the effect.

Journal at the End of the Day

How did this tool work for you today? What happened when you stopped to note your temperature? How did this simple act affect the course of your day?

RED Hot Power Tool #12: Restating

*"The difference between **can** and **cannot** are only three letters. Three letters that determine your life's direction." Remez Sasson*

The restating tool is much like the reframing tool. However, it is used with much less effort and is meant to help out when you catch yourself saying something negative. Whereas the reframing tool is more for thoughts, the restating tool is used for verbal statements.

How It Works

Let's say you catch yourself saying something negative.

Say out loud, **"Cancel that. What I really mean is…."**

Here are a couple examples:

- That costs too much. I can't afford it. "Cancel that. What I really mean is that costs more than I want to pay right now." Feel better?

- You kids never line up right. How many times do I have to tell you? "Cancel that. What I really mean is I love it when you kids line up in a straight line under the lights! Yeah, like that!!"

By the way, you can tell when your statement is negative because your voice will be strained and you will not feel joy. You may even feel angry, frustrated, overwhelmed, powerless, etc. It also helps to take a clearing breath before you start with the "cancel that."

I recall how difficult it was for me to use this tool at first. Noticing the negative comments was challenging, but knowing how to restate them was the hard part. I either came up with some lame statement that I did not believe, or I just gave up and proclaimed the situation hopeless.

Finally, one day, I decided to try a systematic approach to ease myself into a more effective transition from negative to positive. I decided to start by restating what I heard other people saying. I got my notepad ready to carry with me in my pocket. The plan was to write down the negative statements I heard that day and then think about them and restate them. The void of personal, emotional attachment would be easier to manage. I planned to start off with ten statements.

This was much easier than I had anticipated. I easily got my first ten statements before 7:15 am by visiting the teacher workroom to make photocopies before my morning duty. The students were not even in the building yet. I did not even have to engage in conversation.

Just listening, I heard such comments as:

This machine never works.

I should have stayed home today.

I don't know how they expect these kids to pass this test.

They are so low.

This is too hard for them.

They are not ready for this.

There are five people out today and they better not tell me to sub again.

I never get my planning time.

There is no way I am getting stuck with Ms. Johnson's lunch duty again.

That cafeteria is a hot mess.

Jeez, it's gonna be friggin' cold out there on bus duty today.

OMG! See what I mean?

I continued to listen during my morning duty at the metal detector. It did not get any better just because kids were entering the building for the next day of the rest of their life as life-long learners. I noted various repeated versions of the same statements meant to "set the tone" for the beginning of the day.

Stop pushing.

People, you are not unzipping your bags.

No hoodies.

No sagging.

If you don't stop crowding, you can't come in.

And my favorite:

STOP YELLING!

It was not just the adults. We had infected our young as well. I heard them shouting angrily to each other as they pushed and shoved their way through the halls from the cafeteria to class after breakfast.

Get out of my way, n-----.

What you say you fat ho?

Yo mamma a ho, and she ugly too.

I not going to Mr. Harp's today. That b---- kicked me out yesterday and called my mamma.

I hate this school.

Only 7:45 and I was surrounded by a sea of negative talk. If I listened much longer, I knew I would drown. Looking back, it was necessary to feel this overwhelmed. It drove home one brutally refreshing point. It had to get better!

I entered my classroom and in one vigilant moment, I declared this "Restatement Day."

I marched deliberately to the blank whiteboard on the side wall of the classroom. Rather dramatically, I drew a red marker line down the middle of the board. On the top left, I wrote "Negative Statements." On the top right, I wrote, "Restatements."

The students hushed wondering what would follow. I said, "Pick up your notebooks and be seated." Several of the rowdy boys started pushing each other to get their notebooks from the crate. I said, "Stop pushing! Oops!" I walked to the side board and recorded.

(Stop pushing) on the left. (Take turns at the crate, please) on the right.

The pushing ceased.

A little pleased, I stated, "Don't forget to sharpen your pencils, you won't..." I stopped and turned back to the board. (Don't forget...) on the left and (Remember to sharpen your pencils now) on the right.

A few students giggled. I couldn't help smiling and chuckling with them. This was fun. I asked them, "So, what do you think I am doing?"

"You're trying to be positive!" piped up Tiffany.

I had them, and I launched into my lesson. They hung on my every word, waiting for me to slip. I chose my words very carefully. It got easier and easier. The kids sensed this and it was up to Toby to challenge my skill. He deliberately rose out of his seat, snatched his buddy's paper, balled it up noisily, and darted across the room to attempt a crowd-pleasing lay-up shot into the trash can two feet from where I was instructing the class. He missed his shot and fell dramatically defeated to the floor shouting out, "Dang!"

The class burst out laughing. I motioned to him with the come-hither pointer finger, and he followed me to the side board.

"I won't tell you what I used to think, but this is what I would have said," I told him.

(Stop disturbing the class! If you don't sit down right now, I am calling your mother) on the left, and (I appreciate it when you listen and participate! When we finish our work we will ball up our scratch paper and shoot ceremonial shots into the trash can! Woo hoo!) on the right.

"That's what I'm talking 'bout, Ms. C!" approved Toby. We high-fived and he returned to his seat. I forgot to mention that this class was "one of those dreaded classes." This day marked the beginning of a turn-around. It wasn't perfect and easy and la la la from there on, but it got better. The tide had turned and the lifeboat was in sight.

Do It

Listen for your opportunities to use the tool.

You may catch yourself before the words even come out. If this happens, skip the "cancel that" and just get on to the positive statement!

You may hear other people stating negatively. It's okay to cancel for them and restate in your own head.

Journal at the End of the Day

Describe how you used this tool. What effect did it have on other people when you used it?

How do you want your students to use this tool?

RED Hot Power Tool #13: Just Say YES

"When can'ts turn to cans,dreams become plans." Anonymous

Don't eat that chocolate.

Don't get out of your seat.

Don't think about purple pandas.

Don't read the next line.

Why are you reading this line? I mean it!

Don't read the next line!!

You are still reading, aren't you?

Your brain can't help it. Your non-conscious mind is taking the commands and performing them.

It focuses on the command and ignores the "not."

Telling people what "not to do" is ineffective and counter-productive.

Instead, tell people what you want them to do.

How It Works

What you focus on, you get more of. So, instead of giving attention to what you do not want, give attention to what you do want. This sounds so simple, yet if you listen to your own speech, you will discover something puzzling.

Much of what you say is contrary to what you really want. Much of what you say is focused on the exact opposite of what you want. Listen to your comments for just one hour of normal conversation and you will note the surprising amount of times you use negative words such as no, not, don't, won't, can't, etc.

You can change this, and when you do, just watch what happens!

One thing that used to irk me was the way that kids came to middle school preconditioned to ignore homework. At the end of every class, I assigned it dutifully. At the beginning of every class, I checked it dutifully. Every night, my students ignored it dutifully. I warned them. I threatened them. I scolded them. I lowered grades. I called parents. I even tried to make homework fun. It didn't matter if it was hard or easy. My students still just said NO to homework.

One day, I decided to have it out with my seventh grade math class and get to the bottom of this homework issue. Did they ever surprise me! I was totally unprepared for their response.

"Why you trippin' Ms. C? Don't you know 'Black Folk' don't do no homework?" The class broke out laughing. My jaw dropped. The class quickly quieted. It was the kind of quiet they got when they wanted to see what I would do next.

I couldn't help myself. Something took over and I blurted out, "Who told you that? And why didn't they tell me? And they need to tell your parents." The class broke out in a fresh bout of laughter. This was a better, more comfortable laughter than before.

"Yeah," I continued as I snatched a copy of Marzano's Handbook for Classroom Instruction that Works. "This guy, Marzano, did all this research on what makes kids learn. He found out that there are nine big strategies that improve student achievement. Guess what? Homework is number four on that list. I bet they didn't tell him about you guys either. I bet Marzano doesn't know 'Black Folk' don't do no homework!"

I wanted to laugh, but they just stared at me as my logic sank in. I stared back. Joseph couldn't stand silence. "So, is that why you always tryin' to make us do homework?"

"Yes, Joseph, but there's more. You are doing all those other eight things. They happen right here in class. But I cannot make you do homework. That's the one thing in your control, and you have to decide to do it for yourself. You guys are telling me now that you are saying *no,* and you *don't* do homework. It's like you're saying no to yourself, that you don't want to learn. What else are you saying no to?

I paused again to let it sink in. In the silence, I remembered something I had written about eliminating negative words to attract what you really wanted. I went to the board and drew a big circle. Inside the circle I wrote the words:

No

Don't

Can't

Won't

Then I drew a line across the circle crossing through the words.

I turned to face them and said. "These words zap your power to be bigger, better, and stronger. Let's play a game for the rest of the week. Every time we catch these words coming out, we will stop and restate. We will turn our words around to say something positive instead."

Of course, someone piped up, "Is this our homework too?" I couldn't resist. I had to say it. "Well, yeah, but I thought 'Black Folk' don't do no..."

"Oooo, Ms. C! You gotta rephrase that!" Chimeka caught me.

"Oh, you are so right! 'Black Folk' always have a choice to do their homework."

They all laughed as the fun was just getting started.

Do It

Practice it today. Every time you catch the words "don't, no, doesn't, can't, couldn't, wouldn't, etc." coming out of your mouth, rephrase your statement.

Restate the positive out loud. Then reinforce the habit by writing down the positive statement or repeating the positive statement out loud, three times.

Repeating yourself seems uncomfortable? Try these alternatives:

- Repeat in your head.

- Write it down and repeat it out loud later, when you are alone.

- Do it anyway, and explain to others what you are doing. They may want to join you!

If you do this at school with your students, you can turn it into an experimental experience. Write a paragraph on your board similar to the beginning of this post. After they notice it, challenge them to do the same exercise with you.

Journal at the End of the Day

Write about your experience using this tool. On a scale of one to ten, how easy was it to catch the negative words and turn them around? Did it help you to share the effort with others? How will you use this tool in the future?

RED Hot Power Tool #14: Stop, Breathe, Think

"Breathe. Let go. And remember that this very moment is the only one you know you have for sure." Oprah Winfrey

Gotta fire?

Don't panic.

Stop, drop, and roll.

Gotta crisis?

Don't panic.

Stop, Breathe, Think

How It Works

Any time you feel the strong, negative feelings of a crisis coming on, practice Stop, Breathe, Think.

It works miracles. You know it works when you see it calm out-of-control, tantrum-prone kids in crises.

Yes, kicking, screaming, punching, chair-throwing, spitting, cursing, bulletin-board-ripping, book-chucking five-year-olds.

The hardest part about Stop, Breathe, Think is remembering to use it!

When you do, you will get calming, redirected energy within yourself in a matter of minutes. Then, when you are calm, it begins to magically transfer to the student. You may even catch them breathing along with you.

It works at other times as well. Try it when you're stuck in the middle of hectic traffic. Try it when you come home after a chaotic day at work and you enter a brand new war zone. Try it any time you feel stressed, overwhelmed, or ready to blow off steam. It works.

I first used this tool to calm tantrum-prone kids when I served as a behavior interventionist at an elementary school. The funny thing about using Stop, Breathe, Think on that job was that I wondered who needed it more, the upset child I was trying to calm, or me. Here is an example of what I mean.

One day, I was called to the scene of a classroom catastrophe. When I arrived, the shaken teacher was whisking her frightened first-graders out the door and down the hall to refuge in the Library. Inside the classroom, the principal stood guard, blocking the teacher's computer corner as Hurricane Harry ran wildly around the room tipping over chairs, ripping paper from the bulletin boards, hurling pencils, crayons, glue bottles, books, blocks, puzzle pieces and whatever else he could grab and toss.

Harry, the tiny human cyclone, was upset and everything in his path was subject to his seven-year-old wrath. When he saw me enter, he switched direction and headed straight toward me. I swiftly and silently sized up my resources and moved to action. I spotted his coveted Spiderman jacket hanging on the back of his chair, the only one still standing. I snatched it up and held it as a shield to ward off the flying objects that accompanied kicks, punches, and spitting. "Give me my jacket!"

I used his onslaught to move him toward the least harmful corner of the room, and blocked him in with a pile of pillows. "Whew! Harry," I puffed. "I need to breathe!"

"I don't want to! Go away!" he yelled back. I said nothing, but began to take deep breaths as I continued to apply equal force to the pressure of his body against the pillows. I felt the pounding in my chest slow down. The principal and I exchanged glances. This was Harry's third episode that week.

After a couple of minutes, I spoke again. "I'm ready to do slow breathing, Harry." He pushed harder and shouted, "No! I hate you. Go away!" I breathed again.

This time I started thinking about Harry being calm. He was a sweetie when he wasn't upset. I thought about my own grandson, the most awesome kid alive. As I thought, I gradually released my force against the pillows, and Harry relaxed his pressure. He started to whimper like a wounded puppy. "I can breathe now," he told me. So we did.

The breathing calmed his mind, and he was able to tell me what had upset him. He was able to straighten up the room and make a plan for how he could apologize to his class. Then Harry and I made an agreement that he would come every day to the recovery room to practice calm breathing. That way, he could learn to use it when he first felt signs of stress, and avoid getting so wound up again. It took almost a year before he was able to manage his stress effectively, but the breathing helped. I know that Harry now has a skill that he can use to manage his own behavior the rest of his life.

Do It

Stop

Catch yourself getting worked up or caught in a negative emotion. Tell yourself, "_____, stop and think!"

Breathe

As you hold the thought, breathe. The easiest way I've found is to breathe in through your nose, hold for a count of five, and then blow out through your mouth for a count of three.

Think

Call to mind a thought or image that pleases and calms you. Hold that image or thought in your head for as long as you can. Try to hold it for up to five minutes. Each time you notice it drifting away, call it back to your mind. It's your mind; take control.

Just repeat this until you begin to notice a positive change come over you.

The important thing is to practice it every chance you get until you automatically remember to use it. I also recommend that you teach your students to stop, breathe, think. Watch them remind you to use it! (Maybe you should get good at it first, though!)

Journal at the End of the Day

Write about your experience with this tool. How did it affect you and those around you? When will you use it again? How would you teach students to use this tool, and when would you want them to use it?

RED Hot Power Tool #15: Power Question – "What are they really trying to tell me?"

"Assumptions are the termites of relationships." Henry Winkler

All behavior is communication. So when you find the behavior of another annoying or troublesome, or even downright assaulting, stop and ask this question (in your head or out loud), "What are they really trying to tell me?" That is, what do they really mean?

You will usually find that what they are saying or doing is just a self-preserving tactic that masks a lower-level feeling of unworthiness, frustration, or powerlessness. When you are understanding of where they are coming from, you can relax because it is really not about you. It is more about their perception of themselves in the context of the situation.

Here are a few examples that pop up all the time in a typical math classroom when new or unfamiliar material is introduced to students:

"This is too hard."

"This is stupid."

"This is why I hate this class."

"Why do we have to know this?"

What I have come to understand is that most of the time what they are really saying amounts to:

"I am not smart enough to figure this out."

"I am stupid."

"I don't like things that make me look stupid."

"I am frustrated."

Now, here is a good question to ponder. Do you ever find yourself reacting like this when you're facing a challenge?

"They won't sit down."

"'That class' is my worst class."

"Why can't they just shut up, sit down, do their work, listen, etc?"

"They can't even do fractions. How am I supposed to teach them Algebra?"

What are you really trying to say?

"I feel powerless to make them do what I want them to do."

"I must not be a very good teacher."

"I don't know what to do to help them."

So, use this question tool for clarity.

How It Works

You hear someone complain in a very negative manner in response to something you have said or done.

Stop and ask, "What are they really trying to tell me?"

Respond back to what you think is really bugging them.

Student: *"This sucks. It's too hard."*

(What are they really trying to tell me? *"I don't understand this; I must be stupid. I don't like stuff that makes me feel stupid."*)

You: *"Yeah, I didn't get this at first either."*

   "It would be great to have a magic wand or super powers right now!"

   "Who else is having a good struggle with this?"

   "I remember when you said that about two-step equations, and now you really rock at those!"

I have to thank Joe. He is the one student responsible for helping me refine this tool. Joe always had something grumbly to say, and he always made sure the entire class heard.

One day, I was launching a geometry unit. I was showing the kids some samples of cool string art projects that they would get to do. The samples were completed projects donated by former students. I liked to introduce new units this way to psych the kids up about learning new material. The rest of the class was awestruck, but not Joe. They all wanted to know, "are we gonna make those too?"

Joe interrupted, "Those are stupid. It's sewing. Look, it's just sewing. That's girl stuff."

I thought, What is he really trying to say?

"That looks complicated."

"That looks hard."

"I can't do that."

"I don't want to look stupid trying to do that."

So I said, "Yeah, Joe, you're right. It looks like sewing." I held up a finished project to show them the back side. The thread pattern formed a neat and simple outline of a triangle. I held another up to reveal a circle and another to form a square.

"Wow!" someone said. "That looks easy."

"Yeah," I said, "and look at this one." I held up one more. It was a really detailed one done by a former, notorious student who was still idolized by my current students. I said, "This is Diamond's. You remember Diamond?"

Joe's ears perked up, even though he pretended not to listen. "Pretty cool, huh?" I continued. "Wait until you see the back side."

"Let's see it," they said. Now Joe was sitting up and didn't care that I knew it.

I flipped over the sample, and the class saw the tangled mess of loose ends, knots, and randomly crisscrossing lines.

"Once Diamond gave up on trying to make the backside perfect, he was free to make the front look awesome. I can't wait to see what you guys create with your designs."

A few kids laughed, but Joe said, "Ok, I guess it looks ok."

I told myself what he really meant.

"Ok, Miss C. I guess I can do this if you help me."

Do It

Today, be on the lookout for negative responses from your students.

Ask yourself the power question, "What are they really trying to tell me?"

Then be ready with your comeback line.

Note how it makes you feel and how it makes your students feel.

Journal at the End of the Day

Write about at least one time you remembered to ask the power question, "What are they really trying to tell me?" What did the student say? What were they really trying to say? How did you respond to them? How did they react to your response? How will you continue to use this question?

RED Hot Power Tool #16: Power Question – "What can I learn from this?"

"If it doesn't kill you, it will make you stronger, if you learn the lesson." Carl Cordes, Jr.

Every obstacle, EVERY obstacle is a wondrous gift of opportunity to grow and expand. That goes for every problem, conflict, failure, etc. Each seemingly negative factor we encounter is an invitation to come closer to who you really are, a magnificent creature with capabilities beyond your wildest dream.

So, wake up and stop asking, "Why me?" Instead, embrace the negative and ask, "What can I learn from this?"

How It Works

When you notice you are stuck in a problem, a sour conversation, crisis, etc., stop and ask, "What can I learn from this?" Then, mentally or in writing, brainstorm possible answers until you feel your perspective and mood shift.

Just when you think you know everything, life throws you a curve. You find there is always more to learn. Challenges do not stop because you conquered a few. It is as if you live in the center of a circular comfort zone. Each time you break through the circumference, a new and larger zone opens up. This means that you have increased your field of possibility beyond your old comfort zone. Simple math, yes.

A few years ago, I happily accepted a position as a district math coach. This was a next position in a next district. I was really jazzed by the thought of spreading everything I knew to a new land. I was so excited to teach a new batch of teachers all that I knew.

Whoa there. Little did I know I was the one who had lessons in store. Coaching at the district level was an entirely new ball game. No one cared what I knew. No one cared what I could teach them. All they wanted me to do was make them "raise student proficiency." I was okay with that except that everyone wanted me to play *their* game by *their* rules.

Oh, and everyone had their own private rule book full of secret plays, penalties, and methods of scoring. Superintendants, fellow coaches, principals, teachers, students, board members, parents, media, even custodians. They all had rules for me. Rules about what I should, could, and could not do.

All those rules! By the time I figured out which ones to use and when to use them, the **Big Test** was upon us. The grand finale super bowl of the school year came and went. It was the final week of May. Testing was over.

I had to face the cold hard fact that I did not raise student proficiency. I felt like a failure. What had happened? I had to put things into perspective and ask, "What can I learn from this?"

I took a day off to think about this question. I was happy that I had something else to do that day, and I gladly drove my dear old dad to the doctor. There he was, the wisest, kindest man I ever knew sitting in my passenger seat. I did not even tell him what was on my mind. Just being in his presence brought clarity to my mind. I knew I was about to learn something really important.

I watched as receptionists rushed him to sign papers. Instead, he took time to pull out his glasses to read every word on the paper first, and then fumbled around for his own pen with which to sign. They looked at me, and I know they wanted to roll their eyes. He proceeded in his own time, in his own way, on his own terms.

Later, when the doctor advised him to schedule a surgery, he wanted to know his other options. He was not having surgery. It was not in his game plan. His plan was to be at the bedside of his lifetime sweetheart, my mother, holding her hand and tending to her 24/7 needs.

I smiled as he explained to the doctor and told him, "Just patch me up so I can be with my wife. She doesn't have much longer, and I just have to be there with her." I was acutely aware in that moment how his rules were so simple and all about what really mattered.

Driving him back home, I was struck by the fond memory of all the car rides he had given me back and forth to school from first grade clear through college when I had no car. Now, I was in the driver's seat, yet school was still in session. I was still the student.

I dropped him back home and helped him up the steps, into the house, and back to the bedside of his beloved sweetheart. I drove home contemplating what I could learn from this. Be like Dad. Stick to your purpose. Live from your heart. Do what matters. Do life your way. Do it in your time.

There are those who think life is a test. Do you believe this? Or do you think life is just a series of self-paced lessons? If this is true, then instead of asking "How am I doing?" you can ask, "What can I learn from this?" Then, move on to the next glorious lesson.

Do It

Think right now of a current situation that you consider to be a "problem."

Write at the top of a piece of paper, "What can I learn from this?"

Now, brainstorm and write down possible lessons. As you do this, you may discover new perspectives that lead you to new action steps and creative solutions. Yay, You!

Write this question on a card and carry it with you today. When you encounter difficulties, when things don't go your way, ask the question.

You can even share your question with others today. You don't have to tell them the whole story. Just ask them, "Hmmm..., I wonder what I can learn from this?"

Write down *A-has!* or solutions on the back of the card with the question.

Journal at the End of the Day

Pull out your card and copy anything you wrote on the back of it into your journal. Explain in further detail if necessary. What do you think would happen if you asked yourself this question more often?

RED Hot Power Tool #17: Random Act of Kindness

"Once you begin to acknowledge random acts of kindness – both the ones you have received and the ones you have given – you can no longer believe that what you do does not matter."
Dawna Markova

What you say and do does matter. Everyone can call to mind specific incidences when a teacher said or did something that made a huge impact upon their life. That teacher will probably never even know. Now imagine the power you have when you deliberately act in kindness.

How It Works

Your first deliberate random acts of kindness might be more planned and structured. As time goes on and you perform more and more acts, you will become more random and spontaneous in your approach. The main idea is to have fun and remain as anonymous as possible.

An early act of kindness that I received came in the form of good advice from a favorite teacher. It was seventh grade, Mr. Schell's American history class. Mr. Schell was cool and fun. He let us select and conduct projects and treated us with respect. He let us listen to music while we worked. He trusted us and recognized our potential. He gave us classroom jobs.

I remember my job well. I was put in charge of operating the record player. Yes, I was the DJ so to speak, and I was trusted with turning Mr. Schell's favorite artists on and off. One problem. I had no clue what I was doing. We had no record player at home.

In my anguished seventh-grade mind, I was so ashamed. Here I was, lacking an essential social skill and too mortified to ask for help for fear the other kids would find out and laugh at me. While I remained frozen in fear, Jethro Tull sat waiting his turn and Carol King spun round and round.

As if Mr. Schell read my mind, he called me to the side and said, "When I don't know how to do something, I just act like I know what I'm doing until I figure it out. No one ever knows the difference."

This "fake it until you make it" advice gave me the courage I needed to take on that formidable contraption. I would figure it out. As I fumbled around with it, guess what happened?

The cutest boy in the class stepped up to help. He wasn't any better than me! His fiddling turned the speed up too high and Jethro Tull was singing with the Chipmunks. The whole class laughed at the fun, and Mr. Schell just winked.

I am grateful I had a teacher who took the time to recognize and address my personal struggle in an awkward adolescent moment. You have this power too, every day.

Do It

Identify five people in your school with whom you struggle to get along. They could be students, teachers, parents, principals, or anyone else.

For each person you single out, identify three or four positive things you could do to make them smile and ease their day.

Suggestions:

- Offer them a sincere compliment on their work.

- Offer them sincere gratitude for something they do or say.

- Surprise them with coffee or a treat accompanied by an anonymous note.

Next, pick one positive act for each person on your list and complete one action today.

Journal at the End of the Day

Record the change you saw in the people you identified. Record your own feelings about what happened. Be honest. You are talking to yourself.

RED Hot Power Tool #18: Vow of Silence

"Silence is a source of great strength." Lao Tzu

All too often we think we have to use our voice to get attention in the classroom. And if that doesn't work, we think we have to yell. Yeah, raising our voice will work. We just have to be louder than the noise that already exists. Wrong. Challenge yourself to a vow of silence.

How It Works

Make it last at least one hour, two hours, all day? In that time, you are not allowed to use your voice at all to get attention or give directions. You may use any silent gestures. You are even allowed to let others around you know what gestures you will use and how you want them to respond.

If you are using this in class, you may even invite the students to join you. Ask them for suggestions for what gestures will be needed and how they think the gestures should look.

One day, it happened at lunch that I began to dread facing my third-hour class with no audible means of controlling their anticipated rowdiness.

I left the teacher lunchroom a few minutes early and rushed back to my room, scheming all the way. How could I turn this into some educational fun? I thought of making cue cards with directions, but that would take too long.

Instead, I erased the "Do Now" problem from the board and wrote this in its place:

"Today, we will discover how to communicate without our voices. Write down any ideas you have for how we should do this. Be ready to share your ideas with the class. Remember, you will not be using your voice to do this."

The third hour class came in loud and rowdy as usual. I motioned for them to be silent and pointed to the "Do Now." They were curious. Joshua, the class clown, made a mime-like gesture to shush everyone, and then over-exaggerated a tip-toe to his seat.

Jackson raised his hand. He usually blurted out whatever and whenever he pleased, so I assumed he thought this was a good step in the right direction. Then he started, "But what do..." I shook my head emphatically no.

I switched on the overhead projector and handed him a marker. He caught on and wrote, "So how are we supposed to share without talking?"

I wrote back, "Good question. Who has some ideas?" No one volunteered at first. Then, one by one they came forward. We carried on with our overhead projector conversation in writing for about three transparencies. Then, I wrote, "Stop. Write your plans. You have ten minutes. Go!"

They wrote for ten minutes. It was complete silence. You could hear a pin drop. When the time was up, we used our shoulder partners and then our share out.

It was one of those amazing, "high point of your career" kind of experiences. Every kid focused and engaged, respectfully "listening" to the non-speakers. When they finished, the class voted on the best method, which combined white-boarding and hand signals.

Now, we were ready to try it out on some math. I gave them a cooperative task involving area and perimeter. I got such a math teacher high out of the attention they gave each other as they worked in cooperative groups, silently conquering the challenge of communicating the mathematical procedures and concepts.

At the end of the class, the exit ticket was an evaluation of the silent communication method to learn math. It was unanimously rated a five on the one-handed scale! In fact, the next day the students insisted on using voiceless communication again. Of course, I had no objections! Silence was now our source of instructional strength!

Do It

So try this today. Start out with at least one hour of silence. Of course, you may use your voice to instruct, but "mum" is the word for directions and gathering attention.

Journal at the End of the Day

Describe your experience with this tool. How did your students respond? Will you use this tool again?

When would you want students to use this tool?

RED Hot Power Tool #19: DATA – Deliberate Actions to Achieve

"Vision without action is a daydream. Action without vision is a nightmare." Japanese Proverb

"Which came first, the data or the decision?" Kosmic Kiki

Are you letting the wrong "data" drive you?

You look at past data (where you are or where you were).

You set a goal (where you want to be).

You make a strategic plan.

You implement the plan.

You measure where you are, and collect more data.

You repeat the whole process over and over.

How is this working for you? Are you ever reaching your goal? How does this model help you through the implementation process?

Honestly, I never once lost a single pound by keeping track of my weight every day. I never once raised test scores by keeping track of my students' monthly predictive tests. This is the truth.

So, when I read <u>The 4 Disciplines of Execution</u> by Chris McChesney and Sean Covey, I got very excited and developed this tool I am about to share with you!

McChesney and Covey train businesses to use this tool to meet major goals. Instead of focusing on "lag" measures (results), they focus on two or three "lead" measures. The lead measures are those activities most directly connected to achievement of the goal.

So what is this tool, and what does it look like in your classroom? I call this tool DATA.

DATA is Deliberate Actions to Achieve. Stop worrying about how your students stack up. Shift your data scope to start focusing on action. Begin measuring the completion of your actions to move toward your identified goals.

How It Works

Start off with an important goal. Then, identify two or three actions you can take that will make it happen. Plan when you will take these actions, when you will monitor these actions, and how you will monitor these actions. The data you are collecting is now related to the action you are taking, not the status of your targeted goal. Remember, you achieve your goal through action, not measurement!

You don't have direct impact on the outcome, but you do have total control of the actions you take. This is the beauty and power of this tool.

You can increase your motivation by celebrating completion of your identified actions.

So, let's say your goal is to have every student in your class pass with a grade of A, B, or C. This was actually one of my recent goals. I identified three actions I would take.

- On Fridays, I would update my gradebook and identify students who needed tutoring. Then, I would write out invitations to attend tutoring on Tuesday and Thursday of the following week.

- On Mondays, I would pass out invitations and call parents of the kids to be tutored.

- On Tuesdays and Thursdays, I would stay after school and tutor the kids.

I monitored my plan quite simply by writing three words on my board in my office.

- Invite

- Call

- Tutor

As I accomplished each action, I drew a smiley face next to the word. Tutoring got two smiley faces a week.

Did every student invited attend? No. Did I stay on top of who needed help? Yes. Did I keep parents informed? Yes. Did all my students pass? No. Did more of my students pass? Yes. Yes. Yes!

Added bonuses included: Students liked the invitations and began to ask for them even when they did not need them! Students began to take new interest and responsibility for raising their grades.

Do It

Identify a goal that is important to you for today.

Identify two or three actions you can take to accomplish your goal.

When will you take action? When will you monitor the action? How will you monitor the action?

Answer these questions and commit to checking in when you journal in the evening.

Journal at the End of the Day

What data did you collect today? How did measuring your action affect the achievement level of your goal?

RED Hot Power Tool #20: Your RED Hot Spot

"Mrs. Engel was reading to us from <u>The Secret Garden</u>. Does anyone remember that classic children's book? It was written by British author Frances Hodgson Burnett and first published in 1911. I loved being read to and I really loved this story about a little orphan girl named Mary. Mary goes to live with her uncle in the English countryside and, with two new friends, she discovers a lost rose garden that magically heals their lives. <u>The Secret Garden</u> is really about a secret place in each one of us – a place that we can escape to, a place where we can do anything, create anything we want for ourselves. We can make the world come alive, we can create miracles. I, too, had a secret garden that enabled me to deal with the instability of my life, all the places and people I had had to adjust to. I had some crazy experiences as a little boy, some of it abusive and nasty – some of it wonderful and great. I just kept getting new experiences all the time, but somehow I always knew that I could go within and get quiet and be and do anything. I think that knowing had something to do with the way my life has gone – writing 41 books, all about the power of the mind to enable us to be and do, to create anything we want for ourselves." Wayne Dyer

<u>The Secret Garden</u> was a childhood favorite of mine as well, and the summer that I turned 12, I found a wonderfully secluded spot beneath the outstretched arms of a humongous pine tree. Hidden by the long branches, I frequently sought retreat from my clamorous brothers and sisters. Oblivious to the rest of the world, I could read and write and dream and create for hours on end.

Since that summer, I have found many more such quiet spots. I've even learned how to create such a spot in my own mind to relax and recharge my mental, physical, and emotional batteries.

You can do this too. Today, you will create your own "piece of mind."

How It Works

You can create a physical space and/or a mental space where you can be alone with your thoughts. For the physical space, choose a quiet spot in your home or office (or both!) where you can be by yourself. Post favorite photos, artwork, messages and comfortable furniture. Make sure to have a couple of inspiring books and writing materials on hand. Also include plants and candles for a finishing touch.

For the mental spot, just create a mental image of a favorite peaceful area you have visited or would like to visit. Include sights, sounds, scents, tastes, and especially feelings. It might be a sunny beach, a breath-taking waterfall, a quiet mountain stream, or a cozy little porch on a summer day. You decide. Now you have your choice of two spots you can go to when you need to relax for a change of scenery.

Do It

Choose your spot today!

Right now, create your mental spot including:

- Sights

- Sounds

- Tastes

- Scents

- Texture and temperature

- Emotional feelings

Begin the creation of a physical space. We're not talking multipurpose here. Devote a clearly defined space, even if it's just a favorite chair you scoot to a private corner of a room. It's your get-away, so make it suit you.

Journal at the End of the Day

Record the places you selected for your two RED Hot Spots. Explain how and when you plan to use your spots. How would you use this tool with students?

RED Hot Power Tool #21: Magic RED Wand

"Creativity is a magic wand that works two ways. When you set it in action and seek to create something, it does not just [bring] into existence that object or work, it also raises in your heart a dream, a hope, and a will to achieve that creation. And when all else seems lost and steeped in hopelessness, the magic of creativity can still keep you going. For when all else [seems] dark, an urge to create something would still give you an aim to look forward to. And if you just take hold of this urge, it will take hold of you and see you through even the darkest times. Like it did to me."

Jyoti Arora

It's great to have a magic wand to wave and make things the way you want them to be. Sound like a fantasy? Make believe? Trust your imagination and make your own belief.

How It Works

Your magic RED wand is a physical reminder to use your RED hot tools. When you find yourself less than joyful, use your wand. Keep it handy in a place where you see it, and can easily whip it out and use it, even if only in your imagination.

Start out by constructing your wand. Use a red straw or fancy cool stick and attach a star to one end. Decorate with glitter, feathers, ribbon, etc. to make it magically awesome!

When you use your magic RED wand, you can make up a ritual of your own for what to do and say.

Here is an example of how to use your magic RED wand. Wave it once and say, "Abracadabra, I don't want _____, and I do want _____. Yes! I do want _____.

On the second wave, close your eyes and see what you do want. Remember to see yourself in the picture with what you want. The third wave is where you interject strong feelings for what you do want. Say something like, "I am soooo RED Hot and the first thing I am going to do to get _____, is _____. Thank you. Thank you. Thank you!!"

If the third wave is difficult to come up with a first thing action, change that step to the thank you step instead. Sometimes an idea pops into your head, and sometimes it does not. Just have fun and go with the flow of your thoughts and feelings.

If you are shy about whipping out the wand, do it in private.

Do It

Make your own wand out of any available materials. You don't have to make a trip to a hobby store to get just the right fancy materials. (Although, you can if you think it would be deliciously fun!)

Take your wand for a test drive. Try it out on something small you would really like to create today.

Plan at least one more time when you will use your wand today.

Decide where you will store your wand and put it there.

Journal at the End of the Day

Write about the experience with your magic wand. What feelings did it bring out of you? What changes did it bring out around you? How would you use this tool with children? In your classroom?

NEXT STEP

Thank you, friend, for reading my book and putting these tools to use!

By now, after exploring these 21 RED Hot Power Tools, you have most likely figured out that RED Hot Teaching is much more than strategies. RED Hot Teaching is a way of thinking, feeling, being, and creating what you desire in your life and in your classroom. It requires major paradigm shifts.

You probably figured out that the "yuck to yay" happens when you discover and embrace what classroom control is really about. You don't control your class. You gain control of yourself! To turn your awareness and focus on what you are feeling, thinking, saying and doing. You take control of your own power to leverage your feelings, thoughts, words, and actions to get the results you want.

You have probably experienced major shifts already in your thinking and in the way you respond to all the negative situations that occur on a daily basis. Do you now see the power that you hold within your own thinking? Power to move mountains.

Keep this fire burning! Get the support you need now. Join me, Linda Cordes, in the <u>RED Hot Teachers Lounge</u>. When you join, you can continue to grow in knowledge and skill with the 21 Tools and more. More? Yes!

Find out when you join the RED Hot Teachers Lounge Now!

Namaste,

Linda

Extra Tools for Breathing
Do all three!

Extra Tool #1: 5/7 Breathing

Stopping to breathe is a great transition and a highly effective way to calm down before focusing on a mental task.

Here is my absolute favorite breathing exercise because, unlike most other techniques, the out-breath is longer than the in-breath. When you consciously think about the breath count, you activate the "thinking" part of your brain and slow down the random nervous movements of your stressed body.

How It Works

Basically, you use this technique to access your left and right brain connection for energetic, focused thinking.

You will breathe in to a count of five seconds, and breathe out for a seven-second count. Breathe in through your nose and hold, feeling your chest and abdomen fill out. Then, raise your tongue to touch the roof of your mouth, as you blow out, like blowing out birthday candles as you count to seven. As you are blowing out, feel the air leave your body, while your chest and abdomen gently cave in as you release the air. Repeat at least five times.

Do It

Practice right now. Practice the process for five to seven repeats.

Plan right now that you will do this three times today. Choose transition times for best results!

Suggested times to use this for yourself:

- When you wake up in the morning

- When you arrive to school, while sitting in your car before you go into the building

- Between classes

- Before and after PD

- Between lunch break and class

Extra Tool #2: Deep Breathing

Try this exercise to calm your nerves and refocus your energy.

How It Works

Close your eyes. Sit on the floor with crossed legs and your hands down, palms on knees. You may also sit in a chair with your back straight, feet flat on floor, and hands resting palms-down on your thighs. Breathe in through your nose to a count of five in your head. Feel the air coming in and let your tummy expand. Blow the air back out through your mouth to a count of five in your head. Feel the air coming out and let your tummy contract. Repeat at least five times.

Do It

Guiding your class through this breathing exercise:

Tell students, "Today we are going to practice a kind of breathing that will calm our bodies and help us focus our minds to make our teaching and learning easier."

Ask students to quietly rise, push in chairs, and stand behind their chairs. (Speaking in a hushed tone helps set the mood.) Now you will guide them through the exercise. You can use the following words or improvise with your own.

Say:

"Stand with your back straight, feet flat on the floor, and hands resting palms-down on your thighs. Close your eyes softly. (Teacher keeps eyes open!) Breathe in through your nose to a count of five in your head while I count out loud, and feel the air coming in, and let your tummy expand – three, four five. Blow out through your mouth to a count of five in your head while I count out loud. Feel your tummy pushing in – three, four, five." (Repeat at least five times.) On the third or fourth time, just count one to five and leave out the extra words.)

"Now, softly open your eyes. Quietly look at your desk and chair. Pull out your chair and slowly sit down with feet on the floor and hands folded on top of your desk." (As you speak, move slowly and quietly to the area of the room where you will give your next directions and immediately launch them into the next lesson or activity.)

I always say the count out loud until they get the hang of it. I usually start out with my eyes closed and then blink open and closed to make sure they are all actively engaged. Stand by students who will have trouble with this. Try not to interrupt the experience for the many who are on task with you. Deal with the other few at a different time. Maybe they need private help in order to feel comfortable. After we have done it for a month or more, I start to let students lead the counting. Make sure you provide a way for new students to learn it in a comfortable setting, as well.

Good times to do this exercise:

Try it as a transition from a physical to mental activity. Try it when your wigglers start to raise the red flag to warn you they all need a stretch break. Try it before a test or difficult mental task.

Teach it to students at a time when you have their cooperation; use it when they need it. If you teach students to do the sitting version, they can use it on their own any time they need to gain calm and focus. One more really great time to use it is when they run up to you at recess shouting, "She hit me!" and "He pushed me off the swing."

Extra Tool #3: Heart Breathing

Here is a wonderful breathing exercise you'll want to practice daily. You'll also find it helpful any time you feel:

- stressed

- angry

- overwhelmed

- mistreated

- pessimistic, sarcastic or cynical

How It Works

Take three quick cleansing breaths.

Close your eyes and relax your body from head, neck, shoulders, arms, hands, torso, hips, thighs, knees, lower legs, ankles, feet, toes.

Next place your relaxed hands over your heart.

Breathe in and out through your heart. Feel the air particles moving into your heart and expanding it. Hold the breath while you imagine the particles moving around and collecting all the negative yucky stuff, then breath out and feel the yuck releasing from your heart as you exhale.

You may do this while sitting or standing. Keep up the breathing for at least two minutes.

How to Enhance It

If you are angry or upset by another person, or if you are having difficulty with another person's anger, do the following. Imagine a green rainbow of light arching from your heart to the heart of the other person. Imagine your exhales are flushing out good thoughts and vibes across the arch and into the heart of the other person. Your green flushes of good will are so strong that they flush the yuck right out of the other person's heart. Hey, you may not feel you can control the feelings of another. You can control your own feelings and, thus, deflect their negative energy by radiating your own stronger vibe. (And the good guy and gal always prevail!)

You can also send out your own protective intention for good will to surround you in the following way. Imagine a green light glowing from your heart and radiate it outward, surrounding you with a warm green glow. Bask in the glow for one or two minutes with your eyes closed. Throughout your day, imagine this glow surrounding you and shining all around the room. Watch the reaction of others when you do this and note the changes you experience.

Ahhh! Just the thought of doing this today gives me a tingly glow all over!

ABOUT THE AUTHOR

Linda Cordes is teacher, coach, author, and creator of RED Hot Teaching. She has taught math and coached teachers since 1980. Linda has always been a sought-after speaker and coach for her expertise in middle school teaching and instructional coaching. Earlier publications include her book, Teaching Tips to Try, and her test prep materials for Missouri teachers, Math MAP Attack.

Linda noticed early in her career and grew more clearly convinced that traditional, research-based professional development lacked an underlying philosophy necessary to get real results where results mattered the most. The urban students and teachers she worked with were overwhelmed by negative factors that they just couldn't seem to shake long enough to make any significant achievement. This is what inspired her to undertake her own research that led to the development of what is now called RED Hot Teaching.

When she first applied the underlying philosophy of reframing with her teachers, the results were shocking. That year, the teachers doubled math proficiency, and nearly tripled reading and writing proficiency. Something this marvelous and effective had to be developed. So, it is now her passion and purpose to refine and share RED Hot Teaching with as many teachers as possible, here in this book and beyond.

Thanks for investing in you by purchasing this book! Please accept my gifts to you that you can find at the following link.

http://redhotteaching.com/free-stuff

Use this password to unlock your gifts: Ilovefreestuff